Dream

❦

To benefit oneself and to benefit others is like two wings of a bird.

— Zen saying

SPREAD YOUR WINGS AND FLY

❖❖❖

AN ORIGAMI FOLD-AND-TELL

❖❖❖

Mary Chloe Schoolcraft Saunders

Illustrations by Carla McGregor Mihelich

·Possibilities w/MCSS

Albuquerque, New Mexico

Published by:
Possibilities w/MCSS
PMB #156
2400 Rio Grande Boulevard NW
Albuquerque, NM 87104-3222

Editor: Ellen Kleiner
Book design and typography: Christinea Johnson
Cover design and production: Christinea Johnson

Printed in the United States of America on acid-free recycled paper

Publisher's Cataloging-in-Publication Data

Saunders, Mary Chloe Schoolcraft.
    Spread your wings and fly : an origami
    fold-and-tell / Mary Chloe Schoolcraft Saunders ;
    illustrated by Carla McGregor Mihelich. -- 1st ed.
    p. cm.
    SUMMARY: Simple paperfolding instructions
in story form, with a message about self-esteem
and spiritual attunement.
    LCCN: 98-68242
    ISBN: 0-9662892-1-8

    1. Origami--Juvenile literature. I. Mihelich,
Carla McGregor.   II. Title.

TT870.S38 1999   736'.982
                                  QB198-1661

10 9 8 7 6 5 4 3 2 1

⚜⚜⚜

To John with love—

Life with you is a continual unfolding.

Also in loving memory of:

My father, RA Schoolcraft
(1913-1999)

My mother, Barbara Walker Schoolcraft
(1920–1996)

My sister, Frances Anne Schoolcraft
(1958–1993)

My sister, Victoria Lynn Schoolcraft
(1943–1998)

IN GRATITUDE...

I am grateful to the people who have contributed their support,

encouragement, and talents to the creation of this book,

especially Ellen Kleiner, Christinea Johnson, the folks at Blessingway Books, Inc.,

Teresa Goguen Hotchkiss, Dawn Kutz Allen, Merlinda Foreman,

Debra Montano, Scottie Sheehan, the staff and children at

Manzano Day School, and all my origami students.

⚜

PREFACE

This book was written in response to the many requests I have received for my fold-and-tell story of the flapping bird. The flapping bird is a variation on the traditional paper-folding model of the ornamental crane. Whereas the crane symbolizes peace, long life, and prosperity, I like to think of the flapping bird as a symbol of possibilities. It reminds us that any struggle in life holds unlimited possibilities for joy and delight—that when you begin where you are with what you have, you can receive what you desire. Curiously, this promising message springs to life through a simple piece of paper.

My interest in paper folding began when I was about ten years old. It was then that I discovered how challenging origami, the ancient art of paper folding, could be. Right away I saw that the traditional Japanese diagrams skipped important folding steps. Soon afterward I learned that success was not immediate. Indeed, my first origami lesson, presented by my older sister Vickie, ended in utter frustration, impressing upon me how different it is to *teach* a fold than to try to *learn* one.

Not until adulthood did I experience success with the traditional crane model, and later the flapping bird. A simple step-by-step presentation set forth in a currently out-of-print book entitled *Fun Folds* had transformed my former intimidation into invitation, easing me back into the origami experience. At the time, I was working as a speech and language pathologist in public schools. Aware enough to know that success, if properly imparted, can be contagious, I introduced my students to paper folding, only to find that it helped improve their speech and language skills as well as boost their self-esteem.

Students with "learning differences" who often felt defeated in the day-to-day classroom environment seemed to have a natural aptitude for interpreting the simple models, especially if they were accompanied by a story and if the children were already comfortable with basic paper-folding techniques. One fifth grader gained enormous respect when he began teaching classmates his new skill. Months later he "sold" his folded creations at a free enterprise fair. Other students wrote special notes on the wings of their paper birds, which they then offered as gifts.

So it is that the flapping bird adventure, as well as other fold-and-tell quests, originated in an educational setting fifteen years ago. As the months went on, my students and I progressed to more challenging origami models, always through the medium of a story with frequent references to nature, animals, and human interactions. To remain true to the spirit guiding our work, we used the traditional names for some of the folds. The results were not only pleasing to the eye but also academically and emotionally enriching.

In time, the flapping bird made its way to adult correctional facilities and cancer programs. Here the ancient art of paper folding proved to be extremely soothing. It helped participants direct their thoughts as well as focus on peace and healing, perhaps as it was originally intended to do.

The exact origin of the art of paper folding is a mystery. Some sources say it began around the seventh century AD. Although it originated in China, its name—origami—comes from Japan. The Japanese word *ori* means "to fold" and *kami* means "paper." With the joining of the two words, the *k* sound is softened to a *g* sound, resulting in the word pronounced ori-GAH-mee.

When paper was first manufactured, it was a precious commodity used for ceremonial and religious purposes. Origami itself originally appeared in funeral ceremonies and Buddhist shrines, most likely as an offering to deities. Carrying forward this inspiring tradition, I placed a folded bird in my mother's hands at her funeral and gave flapping birds to the guests at my sister Vickie's memorial service.

Following its earliest use in honoring the spiritual world, origami came to serve as a thank-you gift and as an expression of hospitality. Today it is used for everything from calling cards, decorations, bookmarks, and mobiles to personal meditation or prayer, as well as festive and fun paper toys. Currently at home in the West, origami is regarded as a folk art.

To derive the most from this book, begin by immersing yourself in the story and illustrations. When you are ready to fold a flapping bird, find a square piece of paper of any size. My students and I begin with a thin square of typing paper or loose-leaf notebook paper, both of which offer a crisp texture for ease in folding. However, even a piece of recycled wrapping paper or junk mail will do. Then fold along with the story clues, taking as much time as you wish. For added assistance, refer to the step-by-step diagrams at the back of the book. Once you have completed this model a few times, whenever you try it again a quick glance at the diagrams will remind your fingers and brain of the next fold. Although it is possible to learn to fold by heart, it's certainly not necessary.

When you are ready to introduce the flapping bird to a child, follow the procedure outlined above, giving the child a square piece of paper and keeping one for yourself. By age seven, most children are able to fold independently. Younger ones may require hands-on help.

⚜

May you and the children in your world
experience enduring moments of possibility as you fold the flapping bird and set it flying . . .

Here is a piece of paper.
It has a special purpose, as you will see.
You are like this piece of paper,
for you, too, have a special purpose.

Think of two of your
good points and bring
them together.

These are things you like
to do and are good at doing.

Think of two more good points
and bring *them* together.

Remember, these are your talents
and abilities.

Come side to side with someone so you can share ideas.

Coming side to side with others, you'll become stronger.

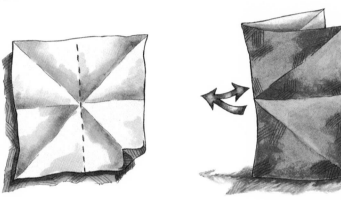

Together, there is so much you can do!

Life is full of mountains—
big ones and small ones.

Life is also full of rivers
and streams.

When you come to these
waterways, lift your sail and set it.

Let the wind fill it, and just
sail along.

While sailing downstream,
you may have wonderful dreams.

Sometimes dreams get squashed,
but that's okay . . .

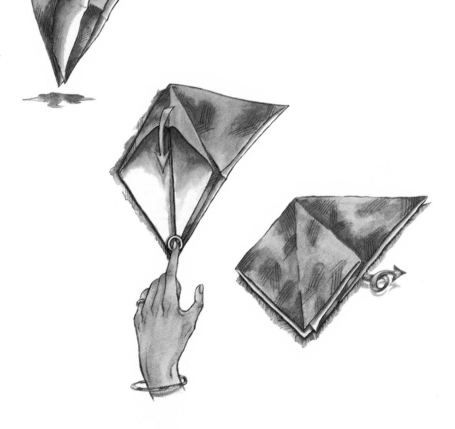

Just pick up another sail.
Then set it, let the wind fill it,
and sail along again.

Sometimes dreams get squashed
all over again, but that's okay.

What counts is not what happens to
you, but rather what you do about it.

Whether you're climbing
mountains or sailing
downstream, try this:

With ears as big as an
elephant's, listen for
encouraging words
like "I love you" or
"You did a good job."

These words are gifts.
Remember to say thank you
when you receive them.

With ears as big as an elephant's,
listen to yourself giving others
encouraging words like
"You are a good friend"
or "I will help you."

Encouraging words are valuable
gifts to give as well as to receive.

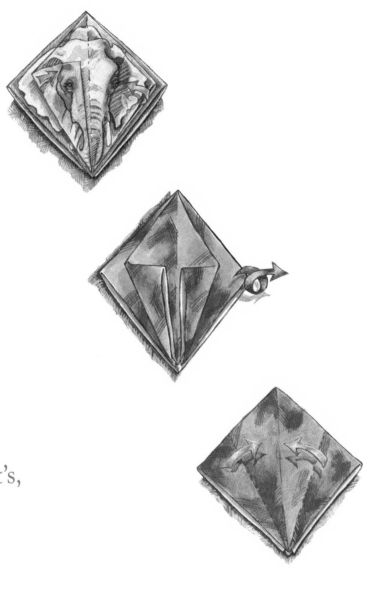

This looks like a kite
reminding you to
let your dreams fly high.

It also looks like an
ice cream cone.

If you lick the scoop of ice cream
too hard, it will fall off. Whoops!

That can be sad . . .
yet there is a happy time
unfolding right around the corner.

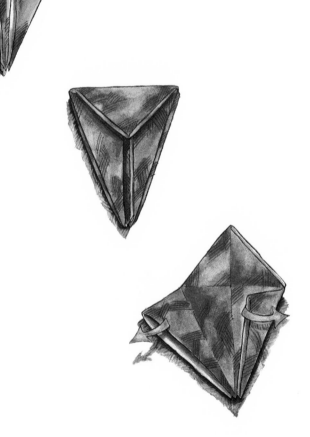

The sounds and sights of
nature will encourage you.

Listen for the song of a bird.

Have you ever seen a baby bird
when its mama brings home food?
It opens its beak so wide . . .

it looks like a canoe

and then a diamond.

Here is another ice cream cone.

If you lick it too hard,
what do you think will happen?
The scoop will fall off the cone.

Remember there's a time for joy and
delight unfolding around the corner.

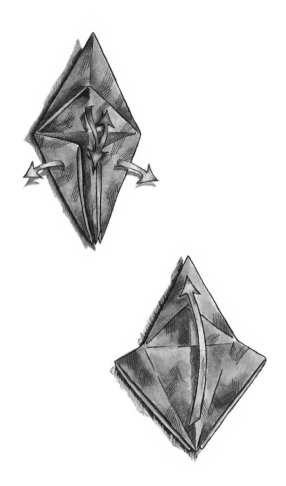

Listen for the bird's song.
Watch papa bird
feed the baby bird.

Look for the canoe.

Float along in life,
just enjoying the ride.

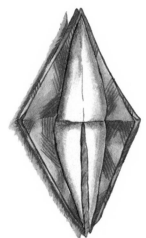

Now here's another
diamond—a most
unusual one.

First of all, it has legs.
It can also sing.
"Dance with life," sings
the diamond. "It will dip
you and spin you, turning you
into something beautiful."

This diamond has pages too,
like a book. Turn a page.

Reading can be fun.
It's a different way of listening.

Turn another page.

Writing can be fun.
It's like talking to someone
who's not there. If you don't
know how to spell a word,
invent it.

Drawing and doodling
are also great fun. Writing,
drawing, and doodling are
different ways of talking.

Do you see the wolf?
Listen to her howl!
She's trying to remind you
that you have a special purpose—
just like the folded paper.

Imagine that this triangle
is a bit like you.

Hold on to your center,
then stick out your neck.
To get anywhere in life
you must stick out your neck.

Now stick out your tail.
That will help you keep
your balance.

See the crown?
You are a queen or a king
of your own thoughts—
good royal thoughts.

Or is it a jester's hat?
A jester is a goofy guy
who makes grumpy old
kings and queens laugh.

That means you, too, must
keep your sense of humor.

Hold your head up high,

Spread your wings . . .

and fly!

AT-A-GLANCE FOLDING INSTRUCTIONS

FOLDING TIPS

❧ Fold on a hard, flat surface. A table or a hardcover book works well.

❧ Make crisp creases; press and slide along each fold.

FOLDING SYMBOLS

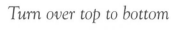 *Turn over side to side*

 Turn over top to bottom

Fold and unfold

◎ *Hold*

◉ *Pinch*

Begin with colored side up.

Fold in half point to point; unfold.

Turn over.

Fold in half point to point; unfold.

Fold in half side to side; unfold.

Fold in half side to side; unfold.

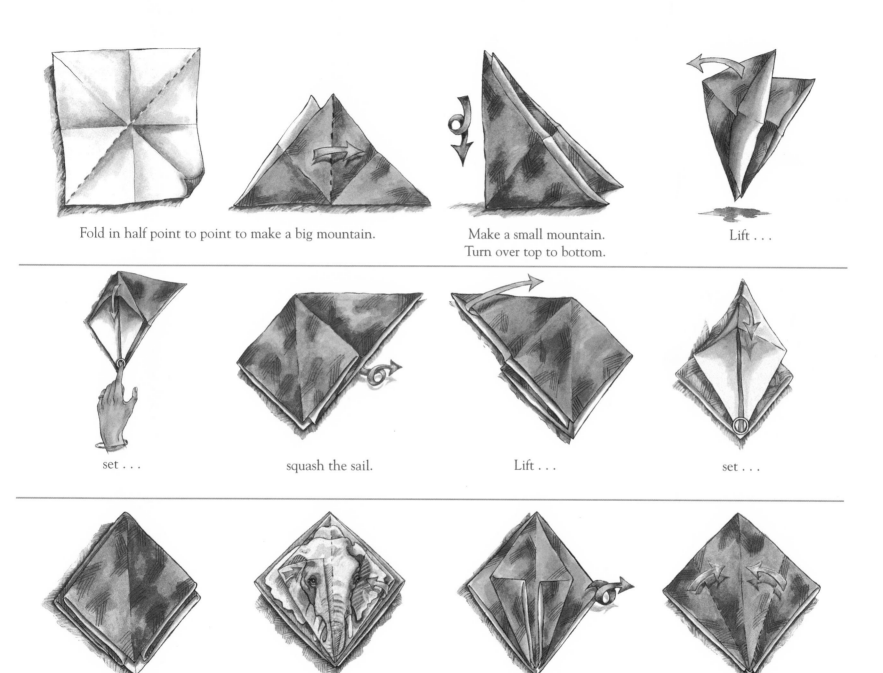

Fold in half point to point to make a big mountain.

Make a small mountain.
Turn over top to bottom.

Lift . . .

set . . .

squash the sail.

Lift . . .

set . . .

squash the sail.　Imagine elephant ears. Fold the open edges to the center.　Turn over.　Fold the open edges to the center.

Imagine an ice cream cone. Fold down the scoop to make it fall.

Press and slide on the top and side edges 3 times.

Unfold open edges from the center.

Imagine a bird beak.

Open it . . . wide.

See the canoe? Flatten it.

Turn it over.

Fold and unfold the scoop. Press and slide on the edge of the cone 3 times. Unfold open edges from the center.

Open the beak . . . wide.

See the canoe?

Flatten it to make a diamond with legs.

Turn a page. Flatten.   Turn over.   See the side with 3 pages? Turn another page. Flatten.   Imagine a wolf.

  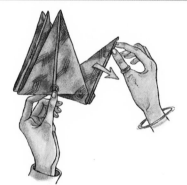 

Fold top jaw up.
Fold back bottom jaw . . .

to look like this.

Hold on to the center.
Pull out the neck. Pinch.

Pull out the tail. Pinch. Fold and
unfold the head, front and back.

Push the head over and down.

Spread the wings. Pull the tail . . .

and fly.

Mary Chloe Schoolcraft Saunders ✣ *Carla McGregor Mihelich*

ABOUT THE AUTHOR

Mary Chloe Schoolcraft Saunders holds a master's degree in education. While serving as an elementary school speech-language pathologist for eleven years, she used origami to foster the development of speech and language skills, quickly discovering that it nurtures spiritual growth as well. She delights in teaching through origami, and augments her presentations with costumes, props, and original songs. Mary lives in Albuquerque, New Mexico, with her artist husband, John Saunders, and a menagerie of dogs and cats.

ABOUT THE ILLUSTRATOR

Carla McGregor Mihelich, born in New England, currently resides in New Mexico. She has studied art, philosophy, and sociology in New York City, the San Francisco Bay Area, Europe, India, and most recently, Mexico. A passionate interest in life's diversity, enriched by her experience as a silversmith, deputy sheriff, undercover agent, horse trainer and dealer, art teacher, and fiber artist, instills her art with a sense of wonder. Carla's work as a fine artist has won numerous awards in national juried competitions.

⚜

ORDER FORM

✤

Quantity		Amount
_____	*Spread Your Wings and Fly: An Origami Fold-and-Tell* ($22.00)	_____
_____	**Origami paper pack**—100 sheets of assorted colors, 6" x 6" ($5.00)	_____
_____	**Origami kit**—68 sheets of assorted colors, textures, and sizes, plus instruction book for more than 20 models; skill level from beginning to intermediate ($13.00)	_____
_____	**Print**—reproduction of cover art signed by the artist 16" x 20" ($40.00)	_____
	Sales tax of 5.8125% for New Mexico residents	_____
	Shipping & handling for book, pack, or kit ($3.00 for first item; $1.50 for each additional item)	_____
	Shipping & handling for print ($7.75 for first item; $4.00 for each additional item)	_____
	Total amount enclosed	_____

Quantity discounts available

Method of payment:
Check or money order enclosed (made payable to Possibilities w/MCSS in US currency only)

❏ MasterCard ❏ VISA # _____*Expiration date* _____
Signature _____
Please photocopy this order form, fill it out, and mail it, together with your name, address, and personal check, money order, or charge-card information, to:

Possibilities w/MCSS
PMB #156, 2400 Rio Grande Boulevard NW
Albuquerque, NM 87104-3222; 505-343-2100

Use this 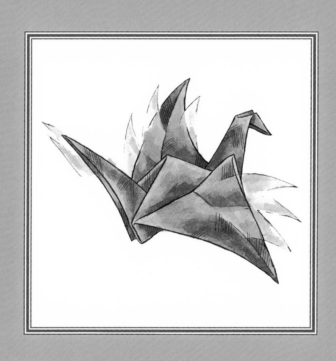 pattern to cut squares of your own.

❦

Dream Fly Dream Fly Dream Fly Dream Fly Dream

Dream Fly Dream Fly Dream Fly Dream Fly Dream Fly Dream

Fly